CW01475903

He Was

TRIBUTES TO HEATHCOTE WILLIAMS

David Erdos

Impromptu Editions

2022

ISBN: 9798848863000

Copyright © by David Erdos

The author asserts his moral right to be identified
as the author of the work.

All rights reserved. No part of this publication may be
reproduced, stored in a retrieval system, or transmitted in any
form or by any means, electronic, mechanical, photocopying,
recording or otherwise without the prior permission of the author.

To Jan Herman, Roy Hutchins, Malcolm Ritchie,
Gerard Bellaart, Richard Adams, Jay Jeff Jones,
Douglas Field, Alan Cox, China Williams,
Lily Williams, Diana Senior, Prue Cooper,
Max Reeves, Jan Woolf, Charlie Gilmour,
Saira Viola, Geoff Francis, Elena Caldera,
Tony Allen, Niall McDevitt, Julie Goldsmith,
Claire Palmer, Nick Victor, Robert Montgomery,
Greta Bellamacina, Heathcote Ruthven,
Tony Palmer, Jonathan Moore, the Memory of
Grey Gowrie, Robin Beste, Henry Woolf,
Harold Pinter, Mike Lesser., and to the Friends
and Grandchildren of Heathcote Williams

HE WAS, AND ALWAYS WILL BE
DE, 2022

Photo of HW by Max Reeves

'As psycho-geographer of the zeitgeist David Erdos has a rich hinterland to draw upon, being himself poet, actor, director, composer, illustrator, musician and critic. The reader soon learns that the writer is well informed on very many levels and that he's in safe hands for what proves to be a rewarding, penetrating and often breath-taking ride. His poems are terrific.'

Heathcote Williams

Contents:

WHAT COMES AFTER H? An Introduction

Poems to:

Retrospective Reviews / Essays on:

WHAT COMES AFTER H?

An Introduction to a collection of tributes to Heathcote Williams

John Henley Heathcote-Williams: prince of poets and squatters everywhere, actor, playwright, activist, conjuror, anarchist, father, lyricist, errant student of the law, grandfather, celebrant, conservationist, painter, Hollywood collaborator, inspirer, paramour and courter of models, musicians, historians and novelists, journalist, polemicist, smooth-voiced sage, cupboard dweller, word-whisperer, trouble and mischief maker, seminalist, rabble rouser, editor, reformed wild man and tarnished saint in the making was also a tribe gatherer of the first order. At his funeral on July 14th 2017, one roamed through a crowd containing every strand of human and artistic endeavour, from famous actors, writers, directors, painters, and musicians, to the children and grandchildren of famous actors, writers, directors, painters and musicians, each shuffling uncertainly, like partly stunned cattle, alongside publishers, Lords, activists, long deposed figures of power and responsibility and more than a headful of what could still be called the lunatic fringe. It was a bewildering day. Nobody could really understand what had happened. Suddenly there was a small wicker coffin lined with blue hearts, and utter disbelief at the fact that this particular totem had toppled and passed into the wind which exists beyond all other weather, borne now, above us, with each attendant name there and status left impossibly small on the ground.

People spoke, wine was drunk, and conversation and clash also featured. At one moment, high laughter, and at another, dispute . People argued and eased, ruffled perhaps at the absence of the connecting thread sewn between them; their devotion and love for a poet who clothed them all with a colour that no funeral suit could subdue. A peacock of a man who often looked as if he had been dressed straight from Oxfam, and yet one whose mind-style and spirit lent that bright summer day extra light. Everyone there had found in him inspiration. What they had done with it scarcely mattered, for the work that he left us surpasses all competition and any misinformed attempt to malign.

As we lined up to read tributes and perform excerpts from his work, we did so against a backdrop of photographs taken across Heathcote's life; from the teenage painter hawking his wares in Piccadilly Circus, to the aging ringmaster of the counter culture, surrounded by the next generation of writers and activists keen to make a similar mark, (while in most cases, only scratching the surface of that ancient cave wall), via defining images from the 1960s and 70s, where his particular torch set stages, streets and bookshops alight with the visceral impact of his poetry and prose, from the '*Mongolian cluster-fuck*' of his play **AC/DC**, to the '*there are some people alive who are never going to die. Put that on the news.*' of **The Immortalist**. We saw a reclining and naked Heathcote Williams, the enviable owner of more than just God's gift for writing, and the older sage, framed by his own startling halo of hair, sat smiling over the trimmed cucumber sandwiches, or fruit and porridge which formed his usual breakfast, lunch, and/or dinner staple, when he remembered, that is, to come down from his writing room to take a little something with his tea. The refinement of his later years connected to a version of a former England which he still somehow represented, despite a life of direct confluence and opposition. He was both English Gentleman and rebel in the same way that the great Vivian Stanshall and Ken Campbell both were; each products of privilege, surburbia and coastal British life, and each forming their own triangle of uniqueness and singularity; products of their own making in every sense, and with their respective works affording the poetry, music and theatre of their time an uncanny power. There were some impressive people at that Oxford wake on that particular day but none of them could quite match these previous contributions. And while some others' reputations may perhaps last longer, none will have quite the same resonance.

It is now a David Bowie-esque five years since Heathcote Williams died and there are many people in each of the successive generations who do not know him or his work. This kind of tragedy happens regularly of course, and while some names become cultural or social signifiers, from JFK to Leonard Cohen to the very young, there are those of us currently tramping the landmines of middle age who wish to set off innumerable explosions of re-engagement and recognition. The Covidian Age if I can call it that, is already being swept under the consciousness carpet, but had he lived Heathcote would have ripped up the floorboards of reportage, opinion, action and art. As a profligate hedonist in his 20s and 30s, his energy, skill and vitriol remained undimmed under the influence of the abstinence of old age and while he couldn't have physically manned the barricades or marched beside the firebrands of defiance who lined the London streets decrying the Brexit Referendums, Unpriti Patel's immigration policy and Putin's current hankering for Stalin's shadow and crown, the poetry he didn't get to write can almost be heard on the wind. His last published books; **Brexit Boris: from Mayor to Nightmare** and **American Porn**, a scripture-like attack on Donald Trump, pointed the way towards what protest literature and art can achieve; a laying out of the facts and a focusing of viewpoint, which contain as much passion and anger as they do wisdom.

I have come across one or two un-versed people, who on first reading Heathcote's work could not always locate the obvious poetry, initially distracted perhaps by his usage of fact and quotation. On one level this is understandable, as poetry is no longer the lingua franca it was in previous centuries. But anyone giving the work more than a cursory glance, will see how

Williams solved this problem by effectively raising the stakes. He made everything in the world around him a subject for poetry as well as making a pure and vital poetry from the world itself. From his haiku on eternity, to his book-long treatise on the peasants revolt, **The Red Dagger**, to his sex-soured lyric for Marianne Faithful's coruscating **Why'dya Do it**? to his finally produced play **The Ruff Tuff Cream Puff Estate Agency**, his poetics encompassed the world. His funeral opened with an excerpt of his own Naxos released recording of **Whale Nation**, and to hear that mellifluous voice, laced with velvet, smoke and gold was to be both reminded and returned to a place of lingusitic possibility and spiritual escalation.

In short, it was the placing of all pieces of information and learning, when set against his astute and near cosmic language and observations that raised anything written to the same level as profundity's highest tower. A writer's sensibility is as important as the words they use and is what essentially draws the reader to them. Heathcote's word-music had a Mozart meets Stravinskyesque impact when it first appeared. By the end of his life he had become more like Debussy or Satie, or even Puccini; with each word choice bursting like bombs of sound-fruit from the page; detonations of sensual imagery, or, tumescences made for the mouth.

This small collection of tributes is a humble attempt to capture the inspiration he provided for me, as a writer, actor, director and teacher, and somebody dedicated to what language can achieve when fully realised. I first came across his plays in the old Henry Pordes bookshop on Charring Cross Road, and much like the generations before me pulling their cars over to the side of the road when The Beatles' **Sergeant Pepper's Lonely Hearts Club Band** was first played on the radio, my mind was blown. From that time on, I scoured every book shop I could reach searching for copies; first finding **AC/DC**, Then **The Immortalist**, **The**

Speakers, Whale Nation, Sacred Elephant, Falling for a Dolphin, Autogeddon, and eventually **The Local Stigmatic** in Penguin's Traverse Theatre plays collection. For over thirty years I collected as much as I could until a chance meeting at the Edinburgh Festival with the luminous Roy Hutchins, Heathcote's close collaborator and the original interpreter of Whale Nation, then performing a new HW selection called **Zanzibar Cats** led to me writing to the man himself. After a life affirming correspondence, Heathcote sent me his latest play **Killing Kit: Elizabeth I and the Murder of Christopher Marlowe**, which I directed on two occasions at the Cockpit Theatre, London in 2014. That first version was a four-hour script in hand fully performed production, rehearsed in two and a half days with a trusted band of actor friends, which became one of the happiest times of my life. After a period of seclusion Heathcote attended the show, accompanied by his daughters China and Lily, and despite some things only having been rehearsed once, and a last-minute replacement, everything clicked into place; from the vibrancy of the language leading the actors into a new levels of energy and interpretation, to my partly improvised live stage soundtrack. At the interval I slipped into the audience space, where Heathcote was still sitting, to gauge his reaction, and check his approval, and his frail hand gripped mine with such strength and conviction that it nearly wrenched my flesh from the bone. In this one moment, I knew that we had least served the standard of inspiration the writing created and that the somewhat painful semi-pilgrimage from Oxford to Baker Street had given him a fresh set of wings with which to make the return journey home. I am still meeting people who attended that night and were as dumbfounded and artistically ignited as we all were that night, and while it does not of course have anywhere near the same impact, or sense of legendary status, as The Sex Pistol's incendiary gig in Manchester in 1976, it stakes a seismic claim on my own life's purpose, and remains something for which I am eternally grateful.

For the next three years we talked two or three times a week on the phone, and I enjoyed a few meetups in London and Oxford (one night when he was confined to a wheelchair, I was his companion and carer on a theatre trip) and I was one of the many lucky recipients of postcards, poems. jokes, books and padded envelopes adorned with his beautifully calligraphic handwriting. It was only at the funeral and subsequent wake that I realised how large the community of recipients was, and of how writing the way and amount he did must have made sleep the very rarest of commodities. Those envelopes, posted at all hours of the day and night across the world, were flags for a Whole Nation of Heathcotians, each as keen to receive a missive from him, as much as we were honoured, and from Portobello to Peshawar, each of us on that strange day in July were crestfallen that this particular post office had closed.

There are no more Lennons, Bowies, Cohens, Keatons, Hendrixes, Stanshalls, Campbells, Nuttals, Pinters, Welles, Kubricks, or Picassos. And there will be no more Heathcote Williamses. The truth is that there never could be, as there was something about the Twentieth Century egg that cracked beyond re-yoking when it gave birth to such figures.

Of the vital artists that remain, from Alan Moore to Paul McCartney, Steven Berkoff, Pete Townshend, Paolo Sorrentino, Kate Bush, and writers and artists like Brian Catling, Andrew Kotting and Iain Sinclair et al, we must continue to pay tribute. They are the last stones on a beach that is already being paved over to make way for a gaudy new pier. We must resist this febrile construction and can remove each suspect rivet by reading, reviewing, and reviving the work, treasuring the stones and pebbles that continue to shine through the dark.

Heathcote Williams was a writer and artist who contained all of society in his work and whose work was for all of society. There

have been attempts to undermine his achievements, but that is
because the true cultural cannibals thrive not in forgotten jungles,
but in the caffeinated extremes of the western world, as each new
generations re-fleshes from the bones of the last. It happened to BS
Johnson, Paul Ableman, Rodney Ackland, and the harshly
neglected Edward Bond, Howard Barker, Snoo Wilson and David
Rudkin, and it will happen to Martin Amis, Ian McEwen and
Peter Ackroyd in due course, but as each ocean wave washes
another away, the drift also broadens in order to encompass not
only the surface, but all of the substance beneath. John Henley
Heathcote-Williams exemplified artist as ocean. And yet his tide is
still turning. Let his work now also cover 70% of the Earth. His
words are the storm and the becalmed, stirring sea.

And so nothing quite comes after H.

David Erdos,
London, 26/7/22

Poems to

FIVE YEARS AND COUNTING

I missed your deathday this year, ensnared as I was
In pet projects. But I will write to you again on your birthday
And as I do now, bound by touch

                              of thought

To the keys and in the smoke and stir
Of creation, in which you always fired the kind of flame
Art can clutch. Just as you did to life, until your last moment,

Which you would have rhymed, Heathcote with all
Of the fast times before; the days of action and verve
In which you shook buildings from chimney stack

To foundation stone, seeking a Huxley-like open door.
From Beiles to Burroughs you roused, from BS Johnson
To Beckett, from Percy Bysshe Shelley to Pinter,

You were the Wolf Henry housed, writing AC/DC
While ensconced in his and Susan's Sloan Square walk-in
Wardrobe, filling a Victorian ledger with the psychedelic

Stains drugs caroused. Grand book closed far too soon,
You are now a work of translation. The words you left
Welding onto and through memory. As we think of you now

We renew the force your form gifted. We, the still grounded
Are landlords keen to give your shade tenancy. Where are you?
Write soon. Sign a slow, sly cloud. Colour rainfall.

Whisper to the wind that stacks stanzas like a column of air
On gnarled trees, whose branches I pass, thinking of your hands
At the writing, as if in each park, street and garden, you were

Reaching out ceaselessly, to shape what we see,
While encouraging a new way to express it, in which
Reach rhymed with reason and in which death

In the very best sense meant release. It has been five years
And you are in the same place as Merlin, another past,
Cast magician who is sleeping now under earth

While being part of it, to stir on, as the buried waters
Beneath river England, moving through soil and rewriting
The Kingdom we thought was lost, to seek worth.

You are now part of that change, whether as dust,
Or as spirit. Five years on I think of you, as I did as a child,
As a myth. And then as a man I got my grail and befriended

You: one of my first inspirations. Today, the legend lives on.
We still love you. The scope of our embrace is galactic.
It is as high as the sky. Arms are open.

Look, they are as wide as the world.

Feel that width.

26/7/22

HEATHCOTE WILLIAMS' HANDS

Those particular hands wrote returns. They were Heathcote Williams',
Living. Now, he has gone there is no-one with quite the same genius

At the brink. He was a wizard with words, becoming both muse
And magus to successive generations of others. His magick begat

Fevered pens, each one of them aching to write in his wake,
Or take ink — from the shadow he stretched across song, book

And poem; for him each city state revolved like a record that his
Evolving verse soon made backing track. He sang for all storms,

His quick quill quelled insurrection and his swift connect
With the cosmos re-rendered shining stars across black.

In the changing cities he left, having done so much
To support them, from Freedonia down to Cornwall,

Via Oxford of course, and now death, he foresaw both
Heaven and Hell, a Whale Nationstate, *Autogeddon*,

Royal Babylons ravaged, and the murders and masques
With each breath. He would have solved Covid for sure;

Author as Architect redesigning, a poemed place
Where word towers Babel for all, sound and sense.

HOW THE HEART LIFTS

On JUGGLING GHOSTS by Heathcote Williams
(Open Head Press 2022)

Kubrick and Welles made twelve films. Heathcote Williams,
Many; as actor and poet, where every line 'cinemas'
Idea, image, thought, experience and reflection,
As is proved in these dozen pamphlets in which every
                              Recollection sees far

Into both future and past, where we re-encounter
The writers who peopled the places where this Poet Sage
Claimed the stage, that he took everywhere, as John Henry
Was left behind to cast Heathcote, seminal activist,
And inspirer, but adventurer first, for the page.

Juggling Ghosts as a set, is a proper love project.
Produced by John Henley Heathcote Williams' sister,
Prue Cooper, his daughters China and Lily, and
Richard Adams of the Open Head Press, the heart's bared,
As it forms a tribute to him through those he apprises,

As well as celebrating the writing which five years on
Gives death dare. Beautifully bound, we can read the poetic
Essays H scored across his favourite subjects for portrait:
Pinter, Beiles, Burroughs, Christophers Marlowe and Smart;
Diogenes of Sinope, and Dylan Thomas, Percy Bysshe Shelley,

Lord Buckley, each addressing the divine information
That helps to make the ignorant more booksmart.
And heart and mind smart as well, as with the visionaries,
William Blake and Alan Turing, each one seeing signals
Through some ecstatic light screen, and then, a beautiful

Tribute to his friend, the much missed and greater
Mike Lesser, a backroom boy who house painted each place
He passed through with both love and wild schemes.
As Prue Cooper does here, for her brother John, the love
Leaping between words as she fills in some of the formative

Forces for us, such as his background in the Law
Which, with severe joy he subverted, to keeping bees
With Monks as a post teen, through to his middle age
Courting of wasps, and the trust that he placed as their
Function and noise, buzzed through the subsequent letters

That he continued to write while still breathing
Until that awful 2017 set full stop. But now, this treasured
Collection restores the Williams words and perspective.
We see William S. Burroughs in London, heroin cure
In his sights, exchanging the spike for the morphine laced

Breathe-eeze cough mixture, and watching Fellini
With Heathcote as the Westbourne Grove bus 23
And its number gives each pen-man their own pause
For fright. Instantly one lives in the world that John Henry
Heathcote Williams thrived in. This is revealed in the essay

On Pinter forming volume 2 of this set. In which
The established Harold, half Hirst, protects Heathcote's
Proto-Spooner, across the No Man's Land of endeavour
In which changing the stage sparks language aflame
A la Webster, and makes the two titans of almost

Shakespearean scope, both well met. And so, H champions
H, who here hands back the favour, alongside
Private details of Harold's son Daniel and his first wife
Vivien. We get to see the greatest writers up close
And primed. None moreso than with Williams watching

Dylan Thomas with his father, the nine-year-old observing
DT Dt-ing, two years before his sad end. And yet Thomas'
Richness of voice surrounded Heathcote's own honeyed
Vocals. Their music and precision underscored his 'eco-logic'
Quartet, of Whale, Elephant, Dolphin and Car:

Have you ever read or heard the recordings?
To do so will soothe you before the savagery is beset
By the elegance of his thought and the artfulness
Of his language. Which he took from Marlowe and Shelley
And perhaps in part from Sinclair; as his piece on Beiles

Has a sense of morality to it, as a mind pushed through
The madness of planting tea leaves in the Sahara,
To arcane window boxes, to dying with all the experience
Of and in a whore's arms, defies care, while melting
The heart as Beiles was also the extreme H. avoided.

And this was a wild boy, whose own exploits often stunned.
But Sinclair's poems were spells summoning new invocations,
For the Olympia press and pre-Gysin, what Burroughs
Then Bowie had begun. Williams' report is detached,
But also persuasive. We come to love Beiles, victim as he was

To life's charge; as was Marlowe of course, Literature's
Greatest missing link, aped by Shakespeare, and as good
As murdered by Elizabeth I as H has it; a gay James Bond-like
Martyr who weaponised writing before his vision was scorched
By Robert Poley's poker, his eyes exchanged for the fire

That met Edward II's arse, and fell from Deptford
Into the Thames set Styx, and death's barge. Lord Buckley
Comes next, another innovator, whose language was music,
From the 'flippishere' onwards, into the Nazz and high hip.
Not so much a benchmark, as the bench on which all writers

Rest on. His work launched and ignited Williams' own:
Words as ship. One starts to see the theme through each text.
As Williams leases language from the dry scope of others
We can see how he saw it sail through these men. And others,
Of course, but these are his twelve disciples to the Christ

Of creation whose privilege H. defends. As did Christopher
Smart wising up around Tyburn, his 'visionary dementia'
Disturbing surface to search for life's pearls while lit
By sea-lanterns; Metaphor's madman, his too, was a soul
Heathcote stored then sets free. The inference of influence

Breaks through, as those who beget breed successors
Who in turn pass the fire that can even singe sea. Smart
And Sinclair were alike, both prone to breakdowns,
As was Heathcote, Prue tells us, as surely minds like these
Crave release. And yet, for each bind, a book that sets

The world turning, and within each book a poem
That becomes its own grail; something for which
We all search, leading us on towards answers,
While the writers that Heathcote has chosen
Shape quest and question in which, as with Beckett,
We get to better ourselves as we fail. Shelley in Oxford
Follows on; Heathcote's next totem. His erudition and fire,
Like mercury flying fleeting beside Lord Byron's clubfoot.
As Corso is quoted; 'Shelley was a sharp Daddy for all,'
And this is how Heathcote frames him, not the chained,

Shelf-stained classic, but the piss and the plenty that pure
Poetic vision first took. His Romanticism not in and of itself,
A style, but rather, a founding spirit; a means to set the world
Moving, passing poetry into health. Heathcote Williams thereby
Became all these men and lived his last years in Oxford.

His brain room in St. Bernard's touched the tall towers
And the spires too, of the verse that has inspired us all
As what he details here becomes brickwork or stones
That shape the colleges and cathedrals from which Percy
Bysshe first found worth. Mike Lesser helped spring

George Blake. He funded IT, worked for NASA, he wrote
Worked, and drank with abandon, He front-lined CND.
He was one hell of a man, battling his own heart and soul
Demons as well as part heaven. He looked for love ceaselessly.
Heathcote said once, 'he was glum because he missed his chum.'

Mike's death marred him. He left two years later, eerily on
The same day. July 1st. The two friends joined in departure.
Mike's was willed. He had woken knowing that he would
With gas make his way. Heathcote's was more broken-breathed,
A result of his emphysema, and yet the two men inhaled

Something that only the heart truly shapes. This is what
Alan Turing knew, too, dying while state-derided,
Poisoning himself with an apple, a twist on temptation
In which all forbidden fruits find their snake. Not a writer,
As such but the poet of course of the programme.

The writer of code and method; the desktop
Oppenheimer perhaps, who Williams works
Into a seismic poem, holder of HAL's hand in an echo,
And founder of the cult of consumers, as freedom is forced
Away by key slaps. Diogenes, the first punk brings us close

To conclusion. Another inspirer, another cartographer
Of the soul brought to print. Seen by Plato no less,
As a wild version of Socrates, we find purchase in the fact
That society has followed the wrong people, always erring
For safety when the wilder way saw truth glint.

The Armies of the Dog encapsulated the step of the angel.
Reduce man down to this essence and in that way attain grace.
Plato wished for reform. Diogenes charted formation.
Heathcote's seminal text now time travels, as if with his magic,
Poem as prize becomes place. Diogenes sought the core.

He saw the soul as a sculpture. Something to shape through
Your living, once you pare down all excess. Williams
Did this, too. He lived on cucumber sandwiches, fruit
And Porridge. He monitored sleep's stored rhythms,
And wrote ceaselessly at all hours seeking the muse's caress.

He was not perfect, by far, as his colourful past clearly details,
But in writing of Sinope, Hackney, Tyburn, Westbourne Grove,
Oxford, Hell, he became his own Blake, a piece for whom
Concludes this collection with its documentary report
On the Tyger and how its anger at us breaks the spell,

Between the natural world and the unnatural one we have
Fashioned. The clothes we wear are skin covers, torn from
The beasts whose birthrights have been repeatedly wronged,
And this is what Bill and co. try to tell us. As Blake fuses
With Shelley and Diogenes in dim light. Which this writing lifts

As the white page blinds with precision. We grow the more
Grateful for what Williams left behind. For as he writes
Of these men, he is writing himself; the ghost juggler,
Still shaping the air for our pleasure and still carving the quest
We must find. These pieces are rare. Befriend someone

Who has them. They are the keys to kept towers.
They are the means to gift sight

　　　　　　　　　To the blind.

　　　　　　　　　11/5/22

WHALE NOTION

For Heathcote Williams' 80th Birthday

'From Space', or wherever you may be, you look wisely
On this, your former and forsaken ocean, mired as it is now
By oil, and by the pollutants of pride dispensed to destroy
Once pure waters, through which the consciousness
Ascribed to you and the standards long set duly toil.

Heathcote, it has been a time of despair, irrespective
Of the ruination some salvage, or which they assume
Has been salvaged while the corrupted current and course
Still holds sway; and after Global warming's gun has fired,
For a planet at three degrees temperature would have

No Coral reefs left to swim through; with Polar Bears turned
Suicidal, tidal collapse soon outweighs whatever remains
Standing proud, such as your work, which was bearlike:
Noble, wild, savage and purely possessed by a beauty
That exists, like those beasts on far plains.

Across a new paged landscape of white, each thought,
Each fountain pen poured, or quill mark made seemed unholy,
While still staying sacred as you took advantage of acid and ice
To cure pains. In all of our hearts, and in each of our separate
Missions. You were both bear and boundary;

And your oeuvre ocean astounds. It is four years since you left
And the white Bear of thought remains waiting, just as the Whale
In lost water who you famously prized sings your sound.
This is the way then with work which contained the entire world
In it; you become the dream you were chasing, just as those

Bearlike books represent the endangerment we all face
As the waters all rise and Ahabs across the world are advancing,

And the cost of care and protection and the time saved for that care
Has been spent. You were borne away from your words by the torrents
Of death sent to claim you, and so as you become the Whale,

You move freely, away from the world, to that place that exists
Far from us, or under us, or beside us, but which we will never see:
So this notion of you as new myth finds its face. You no longer see
As we see, but there in some sea, and distanced by death,
You are greater. Eighty years on from your birthing,

The 'earthing' idea now finds form. For in forging new worlds
While detailing our own as muse maker you are now
The carrying craft and Ark aiming towards the end of our night
And new dawn. Part of poetry's pride, as with both bear and lion,
Or leopard pack, cheetah as each animal pack pokes man's joke.

Spearing us all, as you swim, eighty today, yet eternal,
Seeking this notional nation I have the audaciousness to invoke.
In which '*From space…the planet is the territory, not of humans,
But of the whale,*' There; I quote you. Pure words returned
To you from the present and for this landmark age.

May future gifts follow on and each birthday allow further
Journeys. And may your work to which those who love it still
Now bear witness to what you're becoming. If this is a modern
Atlantis that's sinking then we, swimming sadly, are waiting
To become as you are now;
$$\qquad\qquad\qquad\text{Star and page.}$$

November 15th 2021

THE FOURTH YEAR

For Heathcote Williams

It should be news that today marks your fourth
Year of departure. For when society loses signals,
Or signposts such as yours, the days warp

Folding in on themselves, without the words
To unravel the mystery of each moment
Or the all too blatant lies behind doors,

And the truth that we are poorer without
The richness and way you delivered, as you sat
In your dotage, fountain pen pouring futures

Onto the calligraphed page with such ease,
That every political pose and every social
Shift achieved scansion, rhyming under you,

The verse surgeon whose equal vision and zeal
Cured disease. Four years ago on this day,
You passed into the page your work fashioned

With all of the lost, last abandon that jackdawed
Away above youth. I knew you older, of course
But for those who loved and lived with you longer

May these annual stokings stir embers that see
Your spirit rise. We seek proof that you ever
Departed at all. For death uses dust to edit

The life and work you left with us.
In this, your eightieth year we're still
Reading and readying too what you write.

So grief composes within as memory
Makes us all poets. And so I write for you, H,
As always small stanzas of love.

Words as light.

July 1st 2021

For Heathcote Williams

For your birthday, just this:
More words spent without you
Across the gulf we stare skywards,
Seeking your shade, shaping years

That remember your tread,
Forever felt close beside us,
Your liquid voice spelt and flowing
And allowing tears their own language

With which to dispel each fresh fear.
We live in difficult days that you
Would have described with such candour
As well as a splendour that only your

Richness of word conjured forth.
Magician, your trick came not from
The disappearance you left us,
But from how you have remained

At the forefront of not only this page
But thought's birth. Each new one
Starts with you. This is your birthday card.
Will you read it? I'll send it anyway,

Heathcote, with a star for a stamp
You're still sought. We kiss you on earth
And watch them spiral and spark
Courted cosmos. From these rooms

Of waiting, your light is still shining.
When we arrive we'll knock for you.
The writer still worshipped.

Author again. Open doors.

November 14th 2020

A HEATHCONNET

On the third anniversary of Heathcote Williams' passing

I write about you a lot. In fact, no more than a month ago,
During Lockdown. But as today marks your last day, now three years
Past, I go on. Mostly to honour the dreams of you I once had,
But latterly as I loved you; what you wrote, gave and inspired remains

An anthem to last: a mind song. That all will continue to sing
Into some scarred and unwarranted time in the future, in which the end
Of days we imagine leads to a further revolt in far night. Where under
Bright moons, the poems you prized onto pages each become

Their own planets, or spectacular suns, scorching, bright. Now, we live
By your light, the friends, fans and family separated. We recognise
What was written is now our anarchistic Bible and code. In this,

You would have blazed, brandished, barked and shepherded
The corrupted herd into darkness. John Henley Heathcote Williams
How we miss you. What death takes remains stolen and we will

never forget what we're owed.

July 1st 2020

HEATHCOTE'S WILL IS THE WAY

Heathcote Williams' personal lockdown occurred
Throughout the final years of his living. The former rake
And Poet Prince of West London, spent those latter days
Unconfined, while remaining mostly in his upstairs room
In Oxford, working away, writing volumes; ecstatic words
That sparked towers of faith and belief for gold times.

His emphysema curtailed, if it didn't cage him, completely,
But with the beauty of his physical form unreflected,
The poem mirrors he made showed what's real.
How he would have raged through all this, denouncing
Trump in a trochee, and Johnson, too. In sharp verses
He'd have had Cummings speared. We would also have had

All the facts, prised and rhymed with each shadow;
Mountains of research crushed to tablets that God
Would have whispered and scored for his ear.
He would have set each heart to full sail as we crested
The seas he set for us; waters to rise and replenish,
As like him, we remained, not prisoners in our homes,

But somewhat wary captives, keen on it all, stilled,
But thriving, as like the Prospero he played, his Word
Island was a truly magical place free from pain.
Heathcote Williams wrote as most breathe,
And he communicated with the countless, as those
He prized and loved received letters and postcards

And calligraphic envelopes every day. When he slept,
I'm not sure, for so many waves brushed his shoreline,
And while counting them he wrote of them and for them, too,
In full sway. With all of the swagger and ease of the once
Wild boy of tamed cities, writing seismic plays inside wardrobes,
This one man psychedelic tore language apart like plump fruit.

He would have exposed the blown heart and let the juices run
Through his writing. As with his beloved Webster and Marlowe,
He lanced each stopped line to bleed truth. We need his voice
More than most and we need him back more than ever.
Tragically for us and his children and his grandchildren too,
We will not. And there are so many others of course,

Who could have set us straight and wrought anthems
Of both change and action; those cosmically caught
Star glazed authors of magic and sound, image, plot;
Indications perhaps, that soon become premonitions.
For the prophecy in a poem is how it elevates from the page.
It is the means of ascent. Sadly this unique man and poet

Ascended, but looking down he looks after the greater
Context now we all face. For life on earth is a draft,
That life beyond is refining. And he was always refined,
Polite, gracious, as the breeding he dared stayed inbred.
So this one vital man and his fountain pen summoned fountains.
His words restore when encountered, either through his

Mellifluous voice, or when read. His written will was the way.
And his spark will always re-ignite our direction. When I think
Of our friend love still rivers, finding him alive, and delivered,
And supernaturally, far from dead. For John Henley Heathcote
Williams was a light that would scour through this cast darkness.
A one man drug, vibe and movement that would have assuaged

Every doubt. He was Man as Day, as every word he wrote
Coloured evenings. He was heat and hope flashing, just like
The lightbulb I once saw him remove from his mouth.
And so, I kiss you, my friend. As all who loved you still
Miss you. Find us again, H. We need you. For now,
A new truth has been written, and as we wait, silenced,

We won't really know how to begin when this ends.
But what I do know is this, that somewhere out there
You'll pass comment. On a manuscript made from Cosmos,
The great poet perfects it: for even in death,

Love defends.

May 23rd 2020

BETWEEN BRIGHT WORLDS

For Heathcote Williams

It is now two years since you passed
But there has been no time spent without you.
Held as you are in the thought light,
The word light shines all the more.

Casting such deep shadow, we write,
Following the lines you left with us;
As our hearts and fingers trace motion
Like a blind man found at truth's door.

One can still read you like Braille,
Rising from the page, superseding
What we might call the pale print of others
As you colour in now from far suns,

What the flesh led to and found
As the captive angel conditions
The wracked heart around it and the stories
You scorched that blood stunned.

All of your energies fused
The surrounding space you engendered.
Friends made in a moment became eternal
Attendees at your court.

Prince of the pen and crowned page,
Your mischief and muse venerated
All of those forced and forfeit
To the crimes of state still enforced.

You freed the spirit, now yours,
Brothers the souls you defended. Whale
And Elephant. Dolphin. Dodo and Tree,
Jesus Christ. As you move from man

Into Myth what we know of you forms
New language with which we will talk
To you and with you again, through
Starlight.
            You will be dancing behind,

Nimble as you were in your 'hey'day,
Your 'wow' zone resplendent, whenever your
Writing and way claimed a mind.
Those still on the planet salute you in love,

Winking our wish through the cosmos,
Broadcasting life's message that yours
Is the path still to find. It used to lead
To Oxford, but now, it stretches on

Beyond Pluto, for wherever God sits
You'll be searching for Alien leads in a Play.
There will be starred graffiti, Comet clear,
Bridging brand new solar systems

As you call into question both creation's
Frame and time's sway. You will be immortally
Moving, far, free, as you redefine
The first nothing, rewriting life and the future

As I sit thinking of you on July the 1st,
Your death day. For Heathcote Williams, alive,
As you continue to be, words are shining.
You have sent summer sun

To speak for you as you remain freedom bound.
We await, each of us, to continue the lessons
You taught us; as our released fires seek you
When our time arrives, trace our sound.

For just three years mark the point in which
You moved behind colour.
Between bright worlds we search for you:
And so I send up this fresh signal flare.

Friends and family blaze.
As thought's fire continues. Love's, too.
We will carry on, as if with you.

Breaching the blue and attempting
To honour you still. That's God's dare.

July 1st 2019

THE FIRST JULY FIRST

For Heathcote Williams

One year has passed and your room
Will contain only your books now and papers,

Squatting no doubt, these lost objects are simply
Seeking your touch. The taste of your thumb

As you licked before scampering through
Flesh-fed pages, that your pen translated

And through a river of words, plumbed
And sucked. Some men become mythical,

While remaining real and true to their children.
And yet to others, clear windows are easily

Glazed by regard. Death of course, is aloof,
Priding itself on its distance, denying us all

Rights to visit, with enforced relocation
It's only visible law and command.

And yet for you, death *is* life
As you remain sat amongst us;

There in the love we have for you
And in the guiding line you still write.

Present in the impossible speech
That will be monologuing your absence,

While in the ghost rooms you continue
To subvert and contain these lost times.

We will continue to suffer and stand
In the still moving shadows you've left us,

Hearing your voice at our shoulder
And naturally thinking why

You had to leave on that day
When those we know are made for you;

As our hands arrange themselves over paper
And the fast word forms, silence cries.

For the failing body can house
A resurgent mind for all ages

Which we must adapt to in stages;
Especially on such a bright day in summer

When loss shines through sunlight,
Or the scratching of cloud

On blue sky.

July 1st 2018

THE HALF-TON HEART

For Heathcote Williams

Newly released from the room
He is now traversing across the far reaches,
Writing no doubt and recording
The astral flame and scorched star.

As behind him, nebulae fold,
His exuberant hair's glazed by comets;
A black hole sucks and blisters
As it wrenches away on God's breast.

His spirit soars on. The red bruise of Mars
Heals beneath him. In this star blood
All planets draw galactic food from cold cuts.
Jupiter's immense majesty.
Then, Saturn's rings, where he dances;

A soft-shoe beatnik shuffle
To a Thomas like rage and whalesong.
Turning now, flying free he hears whales
Call to him from the darkness.

In the shimmer of stars there are dolphins
Winking at him, both fins up.
A sacred elephant speaks, complaining
About a passing spacecraft's warped rattle.

Science fiction's scars are pollutants
Staining the space-fuelled page he now writes.
Those boyish looks, well-worn clothes
Have now become cosmic sails,

Plumes for travel. He supercedes solar systems
In a peacock strut, colours bright.
He is a rainbow in red, iridescent blues,
Golden rivers. Green too, from Nature,

As well as purple and white, primed by sex.
He is the drinks he drank, the food he filched,
The sad planet. The books and the learning
And the magic he gave which won't rest.

And as he is padding now from earth's straw,
He is knit into the universal night
Like god-fabric, blanketing reason
With his half-ton heart and insight.

He will be rewriting death as we speak
And turning it into poems
As his voice and beauty become
In our eyes, fresh starlight.

February 2nd 2018

ON THE FADING OF STARS

An elegy for Heathcote Williams

When one of the great voices fades
The world no longer knows how to listen;
Pictures are splintered and what was clear
In a cloud is wrenched loose.

Shining through it all is the light
That was initially formed to dare darkness;
Prising it open, like malnourished hands
On sweet fruit.

A special man has just died
Who I saw fashion light from his laughter;
A small electric bulb conjured by the dexterous
Hands that wrote spells; dense invocations
Of words and comprehensive poetics.

Erudite exorcisms of the systems and codes
The failed sell. And yet his was always success,
From early days, each endeavour; word photographs
Of the speakers, or, the stigmatics rage below stairs,

Then the spraying of truth across Ladbroke Grove,
Stars and places; the saviour grace for the homeless
Whose continued torrent of language drowned out
Defeat and changed air.

The genius in the room with his fountain pen
And mind water; the source of all rivers
For those who he befriended and loved.
A man whose clear life re-coloured the fog found
In others, crystallising intention before posting

To hell, or above. Heathcote: the journalist
Of the heart, and Poet of the eye,
Whose voice music fused word and meaning

And turned disasters' birds into doves.
From ravens to stars he flew with all
Through his writing. Now that a new
Migration has started, we turn our gaze
Upward, watching the sky that's now his.
We will see the perfect calligraphy of his pen
In those streaks of dawn and torn sunsets.
Let each new thought now be his thought

And our time with him this life's gift.

July 1st 2017

FOR MARLOWE

Photo by kind permission of MAX CROW REEVES

When do the young get to stand with a master?
United by name, theme and time place,
Marlowe Chan-Reeves and Heathcote.

In his Oxford kitchen before
The new and tragically last separation
That has seen the sage leaving

On the Ferryman's salted boat.
Two ages in one, framing and framed
By a father; each passing on to their children

Visual and word messages.
Now there is a visceral sense to the old man's
Smile,and boy's secret, as if each

Now suspected the claiming
Of entirely new energies. One to the real
And now the lost other to aether;

To places that form beyond weather
Or are by design, shaped by it.
Heathcote celebrated Marlowe in **Killing Kit**,

That first writer, who created the classics,
As well as the cult of Shakespeare,
And now Max's son, whatever he does

Shadows poems that have cascaded
From Williams well into Art's Stratosphere.
And so a new play begins in which the young

And the master meet for a moment
And help to frame all that was.
All that is has now changed.

All we knew. All we wanted. A lucky young boy
In a kitchen, there next to real greatness
And in a photograph his Dad made.

October 10th 2016

THE OXFORD MAGIC

For Heathcote Williams on his 75th birthday

What words can contain this lifetime of effort
In which the mutated seeds of his classic schooling
Have altered our vision and re-educated us all?

Firing word spears from his cot, infused first by Dylan
(the true one), then the sixties' squats, The Woolf's
Cupboard, and latterly his Oxford to Uxbridge phonecalls?

At Seventy-five he's undimmed in either word
Or intention. Writer, Actor, Magician, he re-orders
Sight for those closed. So many seminal works,

From **Wet Dreams'** angry word-sperm, bleeding back
To Stigmatics, and starting of course with **The Speakers**
Who initially turned him on as words rose.

I have seen him laugh and exalt before the primacy
Of the present. I have seen him draw an electric light
While still talking from the small return of his mouth.

His is a generous muse and his sacred gift is still giving.
His words and muse are his mind-north, while his maintains
His soul's south. His dazzle, his gaze shrouded in longjohns

And blue denim, remains as diamond sharp as his tread
Is perhaps somewhat dulled. But the mind powers forth,
As does the fountain pen also, as his calligraphic perfection

Artfully restores what's been culled. He writes of a sacred
Time in the past, in which he would have been close to Shelley,
Or to the sanctified Marlowe, banishing Shakespeare

To the box room to sharpen quills and roll folds.
The voice above all who has inspired your heroes
And who spends his days and nights writing

The futures' return from the cold.

For Heathcote, the dream is still in the daytime.
We will do our best to maintain it.

Stre Mashe.

Stay transcendent.

As the light forms around you,
May the air in the room keep you bold.

15th November 2016

Retrospective Reviews/Essays on

ONE HAND ON THE BUTTON, THE OTHER SOMEWHERE ELSE

A response to AMERICAN PORN by Heathcote Williams (Thin Man Press, 2017)

Picture two rooms, if you will. The first is obscene, bedecked in gold and clear plastic. Hung on the walls are false idols, mainly of its inhabitant, I'm quite sure. There are shadows here, too, slick with intrigue and filth, genuflecting, while an unholy light too, is shining, granting the room a shocked glaze. Somewhere in this space, a man is hunched, masturbating; if not physically, then in moments in which nobody near him can see. His eyes are smeared glass, and although they seem to reflect human colours, they are in fact, spermed and clouded as the darkest fantasies bolster up from within. This alien currently squats in Washington's White House, wiping his ass on the flag and leaving cum stains on the American Constitution's curled page.

In the second room, in a comfortable house in God's Oxford, a man who' s been writing for over sixty years wields his pen. He is sat in a room full of books, gathering dust, research, papers, a brain room, you might call it, from which he speaks to the world, usefully. His power comes simply from his means of expression; his way with words and the poems that have captured our age since his youth. He writes every day, tracts of reportage and transmission. He too was a squatter, but one whose point was aimed towards freedom and the rights of the disenfranchised to effectively live anywhere.

Heathcote Williams' AMERICAN PORN, handsomely packaged and published by Susan de Muth's Thin Man Press is the powerful bridge between these two rooms and allows the prospective reader to delve deeper into the moral and mental quagmire that Donald Trump has begat. As I write, a programme is about to start on Channel 4 detailing Trump's origins, coming as he does from a line of crooks, brothel keepers and other exploiters of the human predicament, but you will find all relevant details contained in this vital book and in Williams' coruscating verse all you need to know, if you didn't already, about a man who could well align with any Nostradamic description of the apocalypse you may care to mention.

The title poem channels everyone from the venitian pornographer Amerigo Vespucci, through TS Eliot, Hitler, JFK and onto the great unwashed's need to remain steeped in filth. This reminds us that as long as we resist the waters of truth and guidance we will only ever get the leaders and representatives we deserve. Ignorance is ordure, filth, shit, and Trump is the pig rolling in it. For just as Tony Blair seemed to slot into the initial brief of renewed and youthful energy, and marketed his own Britpop brand of small scale totalitarianism, so Trump has come on his demonic golf cart to knock us all into the deepest and darkest of holes.

Williams warns us that '*saturation coverage of the US election can cause brain damage.*' And so it has proved, not just in its staging, but in the aftershow party from which we are still coming round. The range and scope of the poems are as impressive as ever. Whereas his previous book, *Brexit Boris: From Mayor to Nightmare* was a treatise on that rancid little wannabe despot, as he rolls and wipes his fat arse across the sheets of common sense, this one is an assassination worthy of a grassy knoll, ivory tower and Dumas like gaol window, as words aim towards the restoration of justice, a state of play so pronounced that it becomes the reader's responsibility to initiate.

By taking us across the complete journey of incomprehension, in which the idea of Trump is worse than that of Thatcher still empirically ruling us, to the breathing graves we are all now lying in, this book speaks like no other. Among its varied plethora of exhibits;

A white house fly enters the chamber of privilege and isolation and gains a unique viewpoint on the madnesses on offer:

As a way of examining Trump's approach to anti-terrorism policy, as well as reflecting on previous attitudes, the US President watches Snuff films showing the deaths of Osama Bin Laden and Saddam Hussein to fuel his vigour.

The nature of American films are examined as the search for the truly natural among them becomes an issue of extinction:

The Dalai Llama proves a more effective oppositional force against ISIS, than the American administration where a 'drop of blood shed can grow into lakes,'

And more importantly;

The Pilgrim Fathers are detailed as cannibals unearthing then feeding on the dead.

In this way and across all of this books stanzas and pages, America is seen not as the victim of some media madman's frenzied scourge but as the breeding ground for him. Just as our generalised shallowness accepted Blair and spat Brown back, so the seemingly endless parade of 'yankish' ignorance has created its finest spokesman. Williams' poems show how the need for effective language in the age of idiocy is more important than ever. He fuses quotation, prophecy and examination with highly skilled phrases that permeate and unsettle:

'Was there a pashtun rumi amongst those the drones have crushed?
Was there an urdu Blake whose eyes will never open?
Were there some unwritten dervish poems thermobarbically burned?'

Such phrases effortlessly reveal how the cannibalistic horror of America's beginning has not abated. We consume the flesh of our young on an hourly basis, if not faster than that, paedophilically, militarily, sociologically and in any other way you care to mention. The monster in effigy whose waxwork hair blows needlessly in the wind while showing no acceptable means of adhesion is an emblem of the shallow evils to which we have succumbed. The pornography of despair is more deep rooted than we care to mention. Even a sunny and summer struck day is a slap in the face as it now has Trump in it. It had him before of course, but not to the extent where he could actually do something to truncate those blessed minutes and wrench the wormwood of death from the sky.

In the poem, THANKSGIVING, Williams relates that, '*Thanks to PR the pilgrim Fathers belong not to history but to a quasi-religious ideal...*' and that this has created a holiday 'of the unreal.' This vital book is an attempt to draw us back into reason from the far shores of displacement that the unimaginable events of the last few months have sent us. Unreality is a telling phrase, as, in a sense, nothing is real now. Or if it is, that notion of reality must be constantly tested and re-invented. If real means that we elect or allow to be elected, without really caring, people who have no regard for us and no interest in representing or honouring even our most basic concerns, then the dream that the quantum ideal substantiates, is that we are simply in the wrong universe.

Perhaps somewhere further downstream (or rather in a parallel constantly flowing one), Heathcote Williams now rules over a land of Poets, where manifestos for change obey tidy rhyme schemes and allow the readers as subjects to follow their trajectories clearly. In that universe, the writers of reason and change dominate. Keats and Shelley are there, pointing towards history and the heavens, Byron and Coleridge, also, with Wordsworth and Robert Frost both on their knees looking for worms. Walt Whitman is hungrily eyeing a beautiful young black man in the working fields, while Robert Lowell relaxes with John Berryman as a visiting Dylan Thomas dazzles all in the public bar of a nearby Hotel. Harold Pinter has broken his own rule of thumb and crossed over the pond to exhort and rouse the belligerent into making their positions more steadfast and clear, and Dante is retrospectively enjoyed as an amusing pessimist who missed the utopian sign.

Over here, things aren't as clear cut but we do still have this worthy sage of the fountain pen to at least try and show us what we should think about and how we should view all that is. The specificity of that particular what has never before needed such close perusal. And as ever, Heathcote Williams proves himself to be one of the world's most adept journalists. His eye for detail and the level it reaches is supreme at all times. He knows and details all events and correlations, forging examples and connections from ancient history all the way through to the coming day. Bucolically housed, he is rarely settled. Williams scours landscape and uproots every tree. As Trump golf carts on, Williams walks behind slowly, his gimlet eye ever fixed on the changing colours of blood in the dawn.

From their opposing rooms these men stir. This book binds both together. The oppressive force on the one path, the voice of opposition right here. As the strange trail resumes, the foot on earth marks the gold one. This book is an invaluable guide through the devil's country and to the succubus who is currently ripping the roots of those trees from the soil.

Pornography, if nothing else, passes the time. As we all give suck to the black smoke from the end of this devil's cock, let's hope that somewhere down the line a soothing breast cools our fever and that a gentle touch restores our sense of purpose and place, wrenching us free from the societal gangbang and returning us to some bright saviour's sweet and everlasting embrace.

AMERICAN PORN was the last of Heathcote's books to be published in his lifetime. It now joins the entirety of his vast and seminal output in a continuing volume, open to all intent on and yet to discover him. His is a work that won't end.

April 2019

BALLAD OF A BROKEN HEARTH
On Cycle One of Cardboard Citizens Theatre Company's
HOME TRUTHS SEASON
THE BUNKER THEATRE, LONDON,
MONDAY 24TH APRIL 2017

This Agit-Prop structures the house. Located betwixt and beneath The Menier Chocolate Factory, the Bunker Theatre provides shelter to an exciting array of theatrical arrivals and residencies and the Cardboard Citizens Theatre Company's current Home Truths tenancy proves no exception. Three cycles of three plays will take the venues visitors through a comprehensive overview on current and historic housing policy, uniting and reflecting on human experience and its definition and connection through place. The question raised by the season seems to be to what extent are our satisfactions gained and measured by where and how we live and this is exemplified by the political stylings on offer, that are commenting on the economic and social factors at play today (see what I did there?), along with the provision of alternative perspectives, evident tonight in Sonali Bhattacharyya's view of Slummers in the London of the late 1880's, and Heathcote Williams' (with Sarah Woods') celebration of his own glory days as a Squatter in Chief, alongside Nick Alberry, Tony Allen, and their numerous cohorts, fifty years later.

The Bunker has been styled to promote a feeling of comfortable, freeform habitation. As you walk down the slide from the street of the unjust to the submerged lair of the worthy, chairs and living/performance space greet you with opening arms. Even the bar is set behind a sweet lounge style curtain and a projection screen is reflected making an ideal home for the eye. After an appropriate pause the actors arrive and socialise with each other. The audience are acknowledged and yet clearly kept in their place. This allows us the chance of inclusion without the stress of involvement and the thinking behind this manoeuvre shows us to be in capable hands. The actors fill each part of the space with both gossip and handstands, resembling the elegance of a leopard carefully treading its cage. This slow opening educates an audience about theatre going. This is an activity which requires connection on a different level to the spectator sport of dry entertainment. We will have to think and to listen and sympathise on a human level, separate to the temporary empathy of so much art. The makeshift nature of the productions may be written on cardboard but the legitimacy has the substance of stone and the proper value of flesh.

The actors introduce the season and aims of the project. They inform us as to what we will see and how it will be presented and that the parts will be given out as if just decided, with linking material read and presented, coming as it does from represented characters as well as members of the company. This allows us to feel as creative and indeed as immersed as the players, writers, directors (Caitlin Mcleod and Adrian Jackson), and organisers themselves and shows a level of consideration absent from the self satisfactions of the mainstream theatre, revelling in its own celebrity. This is community theatre in its truest sense; for all, about as many as possible, and interested in reflecting and indeed redefining what a communal, humanistic response truly is.

The first of the three plays on offer Bhattacharyya's *Slummers* is an extremely worthy piece, detailing as it does the struggle of one family of working class hatmakers' residence and need to move from the further reaches of the deprived east end to somewhere further more central. Presented as testimony taking place during an appeal for relocation, it is earnestly played and efficiently written but is certainly the less successful textually, as it calls upon the use of taped interlocution from the unseen judgement panel which comes over in a slightly contrived monotone. Due to the mother's socialist affiliations and nascient activism the appeal is denied but when the surviving daughter and protagonist (wonderfully played by Mariam Hacque) hastily alludes to and reveals an unforseen family tragedy, which while reflective of the time period in which the play is set, unfortunately becomes less convincing to a contemporary audience and to these tired eyes. Agit Prop pieces of this sort do not need to convince on all levels of course and presented alone the play would perhaps have benefitted, but as will be revealed there was simply more going on in the plays that followed, on all levels, which had the effect of leaving the shadows cast by slummers across the lights of time, to be somewhat shallower in nature.

As ever, in my view, sets and backdrops trap or unhealthily anchor a play. Plays are a matter of dramatised decision, enabled by actors, props and light and the fast turnaround of furniture and dressing soon transformed the space after a brief slideshow about rising slum property prices, from 1887, to 1970 and the months after, into the place where the disenfranchised psychedelicised burnouts of the 1960's sought shelter from their warped, purple skies in the post-Rachman and recently Cammell, Pallenberg and Jagger-stained enclaves of Notting Hill.

Heathcote Williams (with Sarah Woods') *The Ruff Tuff Cream Puff Agency* bursts into life as the negotiations, challenges and defiance of this new form of lifestyle are presented. In contrast to the first play there is a real visceral sense of energy on display, from soup to nuts as it were, with the opening moments showing the full range and capabilities of the situation these individuals were presented with and how successfully the unknown and neglected men and women society had discarded imprinted their presence on the settled laps and patios of the known. We see just how effective and efficient the set up was. All Williams' work is informed by research but here his actual life is the resource on offer. There is a famous story from this time concerning Williams and IT's Mike Lesser in the cells at Bow Street Police Station, as a direct result of his politicisation from this period, but now is not the time to tell it. Suffice to say that the supporting material and references to his infamous poem graffiti of the time (Use your Birth Certificate as a Credit Card, Joyless Work gives you Cancer) along with work produced by the Ruff Tuff Puffers tells us of a far more golden time when the value of all that surrounds us was truly and properly known. Williams has written himself out of the play but those in the know will garner that he was one of the prime movers (no pun intended), organising the estate agency and daily pirate radio bulletin, newspaper and network of information that the homeless of the time relied upon.

Like the Jews rejected by the Pharaohs, or everyone and everything else that feel prey to God's great flood strop, those vying for the shelter that Jagger and Richards called for made their pilgrimage to the secularity of these All Saint (ed) Road visionaries. From Pius Alexander to Tony Allen, each of whom are represented here to the waifs, strays and innumerable northern chancers, all were embroiled in the constant fight for resettlement and the affronts proffered towards Rachman like landlords like William Bell, presented here as a mixture between a supercharged Ray Winstone and an anally ravaged circus Lion. As in all of Williams' work, the language courses through the air like jet sprays or fire; it is like hidden chilli in a scone; squatters are referred to as 'unpaid caretakers' and 'spiral dancers,' all of whom pass and go under the sacred name of Wally when challenged by the invasive authorities and recriminations in a deliberate invocation of Spartacus the slave when faced with his Roman oppressors. These inheritors of the hippy aesthetic took that free love for all philosophy and applied to it property and the true rights of man. They squatted to make a point about society and its stranglehold on the poor and the reference to the deserving and underserving poor is telling here, especially as it is a reference also used in Slummers and the preceding introduction. In short it is an arrangement of words that places all of us in direct opposition to our own views on where we are in the society in which we live and where we think the others who live outside of our own capabilities and requirements can be found or located.

These revolutionaries, in using love for the kind of good that moves beyond the pleasures of the flesh and the flower were able to make activism and anarchy its own form of psychedelic, radicalising the streets and air around them. The only unfortunate side of things, other than the fact that the project didn't continue in the same way in perpetuity is that the outside world were not as influenced or as sympathetic as they should have been. When Nick Alberry, Williams, Allen and co, called for the houses along Frestonia Road to become their own nation, they created a closed Eden, only because of the attitude of those looking on it all from afar. Notting Hill and Ladbroke Grove have always offered this potential, from the days of Dickensian Money lenders, African immigrants, recalcitrant hippies to the current Bohos and drug dealers who live if not hand in hand, then certainly mouth to pocket. As Williams tell us, 'Adam and Eve were the first squatters to be evicted from Paradise,' under the auspices of an absentee landlord, and the Ruff Tuff Cream Puff Estate Agency is a much-valued attempt at creating a serpent free landmass of pillars and gates for the free. The play has been brilliantly staged by Adrian Jackson and the full company of actors move through the play taking on various roles, characterisations and accents with a supreme range of skill. The evening reveals Endy McKay as the current queen of accents of vocalisation and Jake Goode, as chief coraller of care and charisma. Mitesh Soni injects humour and energy, while Andre Skeete provides a towering energy. Richard Galloway, David Hartley, Cathy Owen and Faye Wilson show superb levels of versatility, while Caroline Loncq conquers all as a masterful Tony Allen and Mariam Haque essays the second of her three leading roles with a lasting and moving poignancy.

The final play of the evening, Stef Smith's *Back to Back to Back* is a brilliant weaving of the fates and predicaments of two couples living next to each other in South London today. The fortunes of an aspirant construction manager and his newly pregnant wife (played by Hacque and Soni) are balanced by their neighbours, a Manchester born lesbian couple superbly played by Wilson and McKay. As issues of childrearing and rates rise and fall over the course of nine months, so too does the language and style of the writing. At first the supposed naturalism of the dialogue seemed at odds with the stylised poetics of the opening and closing monologues, but these then became seamless conjugations as linguistic refrains led to different conclusions for each property. Simple linking words like 'just' sent us onto different trajectories, while the predicaments faced by the characters echoed each other. This makes for the truer sense of realism, which is the state in which all dramatic literature is truly housed. In this play, as Stef Smith so eloquently states, gentrification leads to segregation; racial, sexual, social, economic and political, as exemplified and represented by an unmoved and abandoned mattress opposite the flats and an unwanted bag of domestic rubbish. 'A fox cries as it fucks' is one of the spectacular sentences that ripple through this play like a nugget of gold in rainwater, as is 'babies to be born among these bricks and breaths; phrases as beautiful as they will be lasting and ones I encourage you to listen to and out for, when you attend this selection of plays. I am sure the other six will be just as effecting, but these two in particular along with the worthiness of the first led to a true evening in the theatre and reminded you just what that theatre is for.

At the end of the show, the collected company performed live trailers for the upcoming plays, a novel conceit, in tune with the current taste for future info, but perhaps taking away slightly from the purity on offer, but Director and Citizen on high, Adrian Jackson is a man of taste and intelligence. If you seek theatrical direction, he will tell you where best you should go.

All plays aspire to a musical form. Cycle one of this project revealed that the real definition of the ballad is one that tells the human story in ways of humanistic sympathy and the poetry of understanding. The Home Truths are calling. Now listen well, through your walls.

FROM CALVARY TO CHEMISTRY —
THE IMMORTALIST BY HEATHCOTE WILLIAMS

October Gallery, London, December 9th 2016

Theatre is a church of ideas. Whether under the glare of old suns primed as they were by Greek judgement, or by the uncomprehending eyes of the present, the theatre should challenge and in an indirect way try to teach. This seminal play, written by Heathcote Williams after conversations with David Solomon and Mike Lesser and informed by notions popularised by Robert Anton Wilson, is one of the richest of his dramatic works and one that certainly struck me as a teenager, pushing at the doors of literature and seeking entrance to the mysterious world of counter cultural viewpoint, whilst easing my way past the sharp weapons of the old avant-garde.

The play takes the form of a television interview with a man who claims to be 278 years old, a little too young for Shakespeare but certainly old enough to have lived through the days of Courbet and the Paris Commune. Frazer's golden bough was something within easy reach of this individual, and as he drops names and experiences across the intervening time period, one becomes aware that this play in particular is a roller coaster ride not just through theories of extended mortality, but through the history of rebellion itself.

In his summary of the issues and aspects that have affected his existence, 278's justifications and deliberate obfuscations abound. They are there to both entrance and bewilder, herding the audience into a fresh new perspective, where they can graze on fields rich with nutrients and stimulation. The bravura nature of the flow of ideas and argument in this seismic encounter, needs a rapid delivery, a semi-frantic yet nevertheless coruscating rim-shot striking journey from word to word-image and then back again towards word. In the production mounted on Friday, December the 9th 2016 at the remarkable enclave of artistry, the October Gallery in Holborn, the approach was more stately than revolutionary. Jack Moylett, whose touching enthusiasm for the play has led to this production here and previously, in Berlin performs 278 as a wise old cove warmed by a low fire. He seeks to mystify and seduce, perhaps aiming for the confident otherworldly twinkle of Patrick Troughtons's Doctor Who, embellished with a dash of William Hartnell's austere stroppery, and his portrayal has a pleasing composure to it. It does not however, quite capture the strangeness, or atmosphere, for want of a better word, that I can detect when reading this theatrical embodiment of survival and imagination, but perhaps that is the point: 278 can, like the aforementioned Tardisian, take on many forms and characteristics, as he seeks to convey all he has witnessed and has to offer. Quite how an actor achieves this remains a mystery: how do we create something truly alien to our own restricted experience?

In many ways, 278 is a reflection of his author's own myth and meaning. Williams' career has been a healthy mix of strident polemicism and poetic entrenchment. He was, is, and will remain the ultimate cult artist, and it is important to honour the eerie glow of his work, as much as you value its contemporary relevance.

The Immortalist is not a play in the conventional sense (but neither are Harold Pinter's, Samuel Beckett's, Caryl Churchill's, or Jim Cartwright's for that matter), it is a theatre essay as event, rippling with successive waves of discourse, conjecture and japery. It crackles with the singe of ideas, from the notion of sublimating your own shit in order to distill immortality's crucial ingredient, Indole, to the idea that death is a lifestyle choice, a fashion statement of the deadly, keen to keep hold on us all.

The psychedelic exuberance of his 1970 masterpiece AC/DC is the play's true begetter. It is The Immortalist's wild older brother, who has defied the conventions of upbringing and expectation and gone out into the world to fuck and be fucked in its myriad corners, before wiping himself clean on the shattered souls of the lost. This play therefore becomes the studious and more refined younger brother, who has learnt from the wayward nature of his sibling, and started to reflect on his exploits with several bright opinions at hand. It is a fast and difficult music but one which soon has us singing as the vitality of Williams' language begs for celebration, and Williams as word magus directs us all through the roar of his song. The best plays aspire to musical levels of delivery and resonance and must be served accordingly. Moylett's easy Irish charm captures some of this music while avoiding some of its strength. Pacing and levels of interpretation could be more closely followed, but placed in their stead, is a delicate sharing, a lulling which certainly embodies the sensualist aspect of Heathcote Williams' life and work, even if it does forego a little of its stridency.

What is wanted on stage is an echo or embodiment of what one receives on reading, a shadowing of Heathcote's laughter, as he whips up and conjures a range of responses that allow us to dance towards death. This vital brew requires the mastery of a conductor with his eye on the prize and a racing driver with his grasp of the clutch, as he veers towards it. We must, over the course of fifty minutes crash through the windscreen of experience in order to renegotiate our place at the wheel. What must be rammed in our faces should be a new weather, designed for the fresh hole before us, igniting the throat and the mind. A signpost subsumed by the road.

The direction of this play is at times, static. 278 and the Interviewer played by an exquisitely voiced Allison Mullin, either sit or stand without further staging and this relative immobility stops us connecting fully with the events described in the text and the emerging situation between the two characters, something that should be shared with us, placing us there as they talk. As the Interviewer comes to understand, sympathise and disagree with the points on offer, she too has a chance to begin a journey, evident in her struggle to grapple with the notions at hand. *'Time is a false alarm…'* *'Analyse. Transcend.'* *'…stimulate a different chemical mandala in your body…'* *'…disobey the alien order..'* Again and again she is given the keys to the chamber. Again and again she refuses to move.

A much sought for conclusion of the play is for 278 and the Interviewer to somehow dematerialise, or transcend in some way, but of course that is not truly the point. It's possible that the figure of 278 could be played by an animated skeleton or Yoda-like, mummified puppet voiced by an actor, or imagined as a combination of darkness, wisdom and devilry, as if Harold Pinter in all of his black eyed glory had fused with the type of acid casualty glimpsed in the party scene of **Midnight Cowboy**, before being glossed by Machen's Great God Pan. 278 is a self-defined god primarily through his defiance. And his rejection of reality as we currently understand it, is what lifts this conversation into a new realm of impact, in which the exchanging of states and extremes of being remains the ultimate goal.

As 278 is gently interrogated, we are encouraged to undergo the various stages of belief, from skepticism to adoration and there is much in this performance that allows that. It does however need tightening. The basic setting of two chairs in front of a hung backdrop featuring a blow-up of the playscript's original cover (of two skeletons in conversation), is used, but was off kilter and compared to the shuffling informal opening did not help establish the appropriate context and atmosphere. The television studio setting is not important as the piece is at heart a conversation in the truest extent of the word; (and no doubt some would argue that my concern also isn't), but when one is presenting ideas and images of this calibre, a level of precision enhances both the understanding of what is shown and more importantly of what is implied afterwards. It could be argued that the last thing theatre needs is elaborate decorative elements of setting. We must instead fill the space with words and their tokenistic magic, especially if they stem from linguistic trickster's of the stamp of Heathcote Williams. Having said that of course, it should be noted that Williams is very much his own postal service in terms of poetic achievement, so that is a task in itself.

What I wanted therefore was a greater sense of involvement and control. There were some affecting moments of commitment when Moylett raged but perhaps in this one-off performance at least, a little too much gentility. Theatre should beguile us as effectively as it transports and affronts us, but I wanted the delivery to lay waste to the doors truth breaks down.

I am not of the mind that message trumps nuance – and indeed the low animal bearing that name makes an appearance in the text, albeit in a slightly heavy-handed way — but I am convinced that the interchange between creative and critical understanding is the point of each performance, and that each theatrical event is a collaboration in the fullest possible sense of that word between actor and audience. The best plays achieve this, and we must not stand (or sit) in their way. Instead, we must each allow for the physical nature of the language to manifest itself in terms of both thought, action, and listening. All theatre is hard work but the real energy, the true energy is hard to capture and one that many actors shy away from. The delivery of a play-text is not set in stone. It is after all, written to take place in the air and the air is forever changeable. The essential truth is the same (we must for instance, continue to keep breathing) but the approaches can vary if the idea is to live. It is vital in this play that the audience believe they are sitting in the same room as someone who has moved through and past the 'black kingdom' and begun to reclaim higher forms.

278's ingenious history of the twentieth century's flirtations with genocide from the '14-18 folk festival' to 'the 39-45' one, leaves us with a view on the flippancy of man's actions. It takes us through the ethereal nature of Timothy Leary or Krishnamurti-type thought via the uses and abuses of Tri- and Di-methyl Tryptamine and a 'messiah like universe' of stopped clocks. Its final statement is one that changed my personal view of what was possible with writing; chiefly how to make the most causal statement the most revelatory. When it arrives here it is highlighted a little too heavily — even by something as simple as a head turn — when it should perhaps take us by surprise and leave us at the door of conversion, but the flavour is still fit to taste:

*'There are people alive now who are not going to die. Put **that** on the news.'*

This last line is perhaps the best of any play I can think of. Its impact to my way of thinking is immeasurable, as it is a statement which totally transforms who we are and how we understand things to be. In 25 syllables, Heathcote Williams provides an unruly haiku of transcendence. It is a line and sequence of thought that demands its own theatre and virtually its own medium. And for me ranks with that other great and fundamental statement of importance, found in Petey's final appeal to Stanley Webber in Pinter's **The Birthday Party**:

'Stanley, don't let them tell you what to do!'

These are commands and acts of word-magic aimed at the strength in us all.

If this production had been played as a recital in the round a deeper sense of sharing would perhaps have been received — though it should be noted that it was received by an audience intensely grateful to hear the play again and to delight in the majesty of language on offer — and this would perhaps have suited the style of Moylett and Mullins' delivery more effectively. By moving slightly away from what I hesitate to call 'certain rules of presentation,' some elements slipped past us. The effect was of missing certain choice pieces of meat — which 278 eats 'if it meets him' — in an ever deepening stew, and yet everyone present was aware that amidst peas and chicken, there were the fine flavours of dazzle and duck still to come.

The best plays endure all presentation. It is how we remember them and receive them, if they play for us is the thing. What was important tonight, was that The Immortalist happened. It was served with love by two actors, with words and ideas to savour, and which gave that artistic air a true taste. The words changed the room and the way we looked at it, sat there. We caught a glimpse of the future and a fresh slant on the past. The world opened up, and asked us to walk straight towards it, and to then truly see it. Our fate was sealed. Our die, cast.

10/12/16

BURNING THE BLOOD

On the 50th anniversary production
of Heathcote Williams' *The Local Stigmatic*
Old Red Lion, 6th May 2016

As Nabokov's long buried story, **The Enchanter,** was to his great novel, **Lolita**, so Heathcote Williams' **The Local Stigmatic** is to his pyschedelic masterpiece, **AC/DC**. Chiefly, the progenitor of a greater glory, but a piece still redolent of the private, scorching flame that birthed it. The title, as in all plays is crucial to its understanding: the local stigmatic is a perfect euphemism to describe the action conveyed beneath it. This new revival staged in the tidy confines of the Old Red Lion Theatre pub in Islington, captures the burn of that flame, but grasps little of its beauty.

The production is short, sharp, and efficiently directed for the limitations of the space, but the director has encouraged his youthful and dedicated young actors to roar and blaze through the piece, doubtless to convey the immediacy of its language and situation, while missing much of the subtleties that lay beneath. The play is concerned with the need to matter to the people and world that surround us and the realisation that when we do not or are found wanting on that account, the only recourse our despair can give us is violent retaliation against anything or anyone close to hand. This means that we need to be led into that predicament and not just thrown or forced; not so we may examine the whys and wherefores in a cold, academic sense, but so we have time to quantify the relevance to our own lives and responses when watching the play.

Two South London dreamers, Graham and Ray, co-exist in a heavily inferred homo-eroticism in clearly reduced circumstances. Both are eager to make their mark on the society that is catching sparks around them. The play was written and set in the mid-1960s, Williams' sophomore effort after his debut novel, *The Speakers* and the text deliciously if economically refers to the downside of those glorious summers. The boys have nothing and nowhere to go. The opening exchange about Graham's experience at the dog track is a bewildering start to a play when reading it for the first time, but it is the key to understanding the problems its protagonists face. When a play gives you sparse stage direction it is because the writing is telling you, consciously or not, that the text is perhaps meant to exist in an internal space. The play is about the fantasies its protagonists face and the antagonisms reality presents them. The lack of safe substance from which to draw interpretation means that all answers must be found *in the text*.

This production starts with a scene setter; pre-recorded sound of the racetrack with Graham improvising his reactions to the race. He swears, struts and swaggers. The house music of popular sixties doom anthems overprepares us for this; The Stones' 'Paint it Black, ' The Animal's 'Please Don't Let Me Be Misunderstood', The Velvet's 'I'm Waiting for the Man, ' so before the play begins, we have been forced down one treeless path of interpretation and it is down that unwavering path we remain.

My own belief as a director is that one has to realise the text and not impose on it. I recognise in saying this, that it is a view not shared by others and that there is nothing wrong in providing audiences with some context, especially those for whom the play is unfamiliar. Indeed, Stigmatic has long been an almost mythic text, rarely performed, published in this country in the long out of print Traverse Plays collection and only recently available in its filmed version on an Al Pacino collection released in the US, as the play, as has been noted elsewhere, has long been a pet project and point of obsession for him. But my point still stands; if you start a play with recorded sound, as many do on the fringe and indeed elsewhere, you begin, in my view, with a *false* moment. When the language and style is as rich and as dense as true theatricality demands — as it is in this play — all you need do is release it, explore it and allow your actors to direct its true focus to those watching, thereby allowing the world and context of the play to be established *through that language*. This observation comes not from criticism but from devotion to the play and what I believe theatre can do. It's all subjective of course but this is what reviews are for and productions also.

What the director, and his cast have done is to paint the scenes in close shades of the same colour. The actors shout and declaim from the 'off' and Graham's desperate vigil at the dog track is then followed by a solitary Ray seeking to attack the armchair and bedsit around him, without provocation and simply as a display of the uncontrolled rage which clearly fuels and infects him. These two impositions, which I name as such because they are not in the text, no doubt allowed the actors to access the energies required to take them through the play but they also rob it of some of its truer sensations. If Graham and Ray are shown to be unbalanced from the start we cannot begin to understand them. Especially when the play is as short as this one. Other reviews have praised the 'What the Fuck' quality of the production. To this, I can only add the belief that 'Why the Fuck' is as important. If theatre is to create a world we need some explanation for it.

There is a pleasing chemistry between the two lead actors, Wilson James and William Frazer, who as young men have all the charm, appeal and swagger a younger audience will appreciate, but swaggering young men can also be a trap door. To sacrifice the notion of their vulnerability and humanity, however warped, is to sacrifice the true horror of recognition. Society's monsters are not cartoons. They are the people drawing the pictures we all crave to look at.

The two young men are followers and proto-stalkers of the famous. At one point, Anna Massey, Shirley-Anne Field and the Duke of Bedford are listed as among Ray's favourites. This shows unbalance to some degree, of course, but the comedic value of the targets is somewhat coarsened by the unrelenting machismo on offer. When the two men confront the target of their attack, a British film actor, David, played by Tom Sawyer, their coquettish display and front are overly exaggerated, almost lampoonish, and therefore the interplay is robbed of subtlety and the chill factor of real disturbance is thawed. Taken at such a pitch of distortion, there is no dramatic reason for David to remain in their company as they proceed to chat him up and ply him with drinks.

In an interview for *The International Times* website, Mr. Toumey related that his favourite line in the play occurred when Graham asks David what he's drinking. When he's told campari, he refers to it as 'port and lemon in disguise, ' and then says, 'you're sewn up, ain'tcha?' If the true coldness of this threat is to be grasped it needs to come from an unexpected place, the result of two outsiders battering their way in from the void, only to find ruins at every quarter.

The 'boys ' have a need and compunction to matter. Attractively dressed and styled, their misfit nature is unexplained but still needs to be legitimised. Ray is always being thrown out of pubs, particularly the *Earl of Strathmore* in Earls Court, a queer pub, whose banning of him, he finds ironic. While this does not imply the Graham and Ray are gay in actuality, there is nothing to substantiate the opposite and when a young woman that Ray is sleeping with is said to be coming round to their flat to visit, Ray quickly decides to 'cut' or cancel her and go out with Graham instead. To my thinking, this adds to the dreamscapes within which the two roam, playing with identities in the same way as immortalised by those compromised celebrities and serial killers, who do not possess any of their own. I was looking for a stumble, but all I found was strut.

Essentially of course, these are small details, but they are transformative ones. A slight unsteadiness would have shown a semblance of dislocation from the confidence of 1960's London happening around them that went some way to explaining why they descend into a state of near murder. I wanted the boys' nervousness, and frailty to seep out through their sweat. A young Shirley Anne Field would pump the blood of any young man in the immediate vicinity and certainly, Anna Massey had her charms, but the *Duke of Bedford*? Instead, with everything pumped up to the max, it all seems a foregone conclusion. What I required was more space given for the ideas and meaning behind the language to breathe. This is particularly important in a small and smoke-tinged room where the observer's mind often lingers on the surface.

Of course, to some extent a one act play does not give you much room to maneuver, but the production uses the cramped space extremely well. It is brilliantly lit by Tom Kitney in its three main areas of bedsit, bar and street for instance, but the point remains: One act plays bare the same relation as short stories do to novels; you may not have the expansion, but you have the subtle shades, the details. To push the analogy into painterly terms: when the canvas is small, you must begin to consider the brush.

I didn't believe the attack on David captured the shock effect of the violence as unravelled by the play. There is a prefiguring scene, when an unnamed *man* interrupts Graham and Ray's nightly walk between pubs. Here, he is blind and lashes out with his cane, forcing the boys into a series of animalistic and stylised movements. When he is persuaded and shouted off, it is done so through a door upstage left on the back wall, and this expands the stage space well. But when David is kicked and beaten by Ray, the actor falls and remains downstage at the feet of the audience. This wouldn't matter so much for the fact that at the end of the scene, the actor leaves, destroying the image and resonance of attack. The intention was clearly to connect the audience to the violence, but if the image is discarded this isn't achieved as fully as it could be if placed elsewhere. Particularly if we are to feel it coming. We already know that it is, through reading or listening to the play, (something audiences rarely do) but when it does, it should shock us with its fury and ugliness. I felt those vital energies were spent before the moment of attack, leaving us with a sense of containment and a lightly stylised series of actions. With the body draped in a coat there is a silent placing and grinding of the foot, first on hip and then crotch, and the facial gouging with a flick knife occurring under the coat receives no movement or scream. I needed volume and shock here and not in the pages and minutes before. I wanted the attack to be on us, as an audience so that we could see the true affects of self-destructive thinking writ large on the man's face or page. The return to the flat which follows therefore forgives or excuses our aggressors, rather than allowing us to see them as the wild and somewhat neglected dogs pushed back into their own cage; dogs who are forced to run their own race against the society around them, which thinks so little of them, that they are not spared even a scrap of attention.

The argument for subtlety in some places allows for savagery in others. Small theatre spaces like the *Old Red Lion* can become immersive, almost cinematic experiences if the levels of delivery are artfully poised.

The production was also song heavy, hammering the isolationist point home somewhat needlessly as it is there in the text. Along with the aforementioned opening salvo, The Kinks' 'I'm not like Everybody Else,' The Walker Brothers, 'The Sun Ain't Gonna Shine Anymore,' The Who's 'The Kid's Are Alright' all underlined an unnecessary literalism. Williams' work has its own music. His is the playlist I would much rather hear.

The young audience enjoyed it greatly on press night, as I'm sure all others did, and that of course is to be celebrated as it gets the play and Williams' name out to new generations. But literature should educate and entertain and to my thinking the production was soaked not in the cold blood of remorse and helplessness of real character, but in the slick oil of the cinematic psycho. Perhaps that's inescapable these days. We've had so many of them after all, from *Friday the 13th* to *Casualty*, but there was a chance here for something else.

The monsters among us commit their atrocities, if not quietly, then with certain levels of discretion and/or lack of control. Perhaps that is not possible in these unenlightened times when we are more than a little distanced from the simple power of the word, but I believe it should still be something to strive for.

At a time when new plays at the fashionable theatres last little more than an hour, *The Local Stigmatic* at 50 minutes is in the truly modern tradition of the One Act Play as defined by Pinter, Bond, Brenton and Snoo Wilson in the sixties. It stands its own ground. I felt that certain decisions in this production has reduced the play rather than expanded it. Here were speakers belting it out in the closed rooms of the oncoming night. I wanted whispers or even moans in those neglected shadows. Wilson James' Graham was in a constant state of committed and unblinking psychopathy from the get-go, but performed with impressive energy and attack. William Frazer's *Ray* had more colour and style but less gradation and modulation in his changing states, and Tom Sawyer's *Man* and *David* were finely wrought studies of persecution if a little over and then underplayed respectively.

This critique is offered with respect for mounting and recognising the anniversary of a seminal play and effectively placing it within a vibrant theatrical context.

I merely wished for a closer scrutiny, which is always the province of a studio theatre; an ability to see the blood within the vein, worrying itself to the skin. True rage and dissatisfaction are cold and can often empty us. Once the fire has cracked, only then does the burning begin.

7th May 2016

TRANSCENDENT COURAGE:
On BADSHAH KHAN ISLAMIC PEACE WARRIOR
by Heathcote Williams

Over fifty years since his first publication, Heathcote Williams continues to chart both the injustices and deeply felt poetics at the heart of the human experience. This masterly new investigative poem is an exemplary study of a neglected Angel on Earth. In writing this book, Mr Williams has continued to create and define a new genre; that of poetic journalism and biography, continuing a series of works including **The Red Dagger**, **Killing Kit**, **The Ruff Tuff Cream Puff Agency**, **David Cameron Eats Kittens**, and his evisceration of the British Monarchy; **Royal Babylon**. Such works draw our attention to predicaments and individuals who necessitate scrutiny. And there is no better example of that than the figure of Peshawar born 'Shah of Shahs' Badshah Khan himself. A close friend and companion of Mahatma Gandhi, this Pashtun 6 foot 5 giant of a man founded an Islamic Peace Army of ten thousand unarmed 'soldiers' while the sectarian conflict that would pull India apart in the late 1940's raged around them.' In the current climate of suspicion and residual fear felt by the West towards the nation and movement of Islam, it goes without saying just how important it is to consider and review the life and work of one of its most positive proponents. The exactitude shown by Williams in this masterly poetic portrayal demonstrates one of his many stunning characteristics as a Writer, Poet, Journalist and Polemicist; the simple ability to educate and enlighten the public's ignorance of some of the darkest and most important areas of its own history.

Born in Afghanistan, Abdul Ghaffar Khan, as the son of a benign tribal Shah, devoted his life to nonviolent protest. It was these actions and stance that this epic poem reflects and dignifies. Categorised by Williams as *'weaponised goodness'*, Khan's defiance of British rule led to a twenty-seven year-long imprisonment — thereby equalling Nelson Mandela's status as an ultimate Prisoner of Conscience for the age, as well as enduring frequent torturing at the hands of the British. A jihad in reverse as we now understand it, but defined by Khan in his lifetime as the spreading of love and understanding between all men. The poem describes how Khan strove to break the 'useless customs' of imperialism and its practises, offering instead only the clear-sighted values of wisdom and equality, thereby unifying all religions by stating that 'belief in God is to love your fellow man.' The brutality that he faced in trying to deliver that message exposes the limitations of not only all of those corrupted in the West, but also those who seek to misread and misrepresent a sense of belonging to and ownership of your own territory. Those on any side willing to use the suffering of others to justify their beliefs are not the soldiers of God, but rather the defenders of their own weakness.

The style of the book is crucial. One of Einstein's concerns in developing the Theory of Relativity was to 'unify the fields.' Heathcote Williams unifies the fields of poetry, biography and journalism effortlessly in this poem, with a writing style that combines extensive research with poetic reflection and contemplation. The result is an active linguistic philosophy: a uniquely considered response to events delivered to us in a language that is both educative and accessible. Williams, one of the great stylists of the 20th Century has developed a poetic voice that simplifies and elucidates. It is a kind of wave populated by the facts and details he wishes to communicate. There is a great deal of reported speech and quotation in the book, which blend seamlessly with the pitch and rise of the narratives presentation of facts. This sensual aspect of Mr Williams' writing is one its major areas of appeal. Anyone familiar with his acting roles in film, or Audiobook recordings will recognise how the smoothness and honeyed rasp of his speaking voice is resonantly echoed in his written one. He is both Teacher and Lawyer, representing the information and accused by his insistent and rigourous examination of his subjects opposing forces, whether they be Khan's postwar British persecutors or the Japanese Whale Hunters, skewered effectively in his iconic **Whale Nation**.

Too often poetry falls prey to trends or indulgence. Williams' work as a whole and this book as its most recent example easily resists that state of affairs. It creates and consolidates its own approach in a seductively measured blank verse style that seeks to dignify and embody the inspirational human being it honours.

Khan's deep understanding of the spiritual response and his spirited defiance of oppression granted him the transcendent courage quoted in the text. His extensive struggle is made all the more relevant by the fact that Afghanistan was the site and subject of his labours. Williams encapsulates the history of this area through his detailing of Khans' endurance, balancing it chillingly with a study of Afghanistan's role as target for the machinations of the American War machine and their attempt to nullify neighbouring Russia's hold over the area. Reagan's warmongery is exposed once more as is Obama's recent pride at his Tuesday Morning Kill List, with former President Clinton's phallic missiles affectionately termed as Lewinsky's giving us the darkest of final laughs. Throughout all of this the purity and character of Khan shines through, showing us that those who represent the culture we espouse are as barbaric and inhumane as our imagined eastern enemy.

The true Prophet is not concerned with religion but simply with the human impulse. In an increasingly ignorant age, history and religion show us that they are questioned, denied or misunderstood far too often. This book and the life it conveys show how the direct prophecies of love and understanding are the most relevant. Making the ill informed understand that is therefore the only true task. Khan offered the means to love and to defend that love honourably. He saw nonviolence in a violent world as the highest form of devotion and asked and suffered at the hands of those only ready to hate. Ghaffar Khan died in 1988 at the age of 98, a near century of life that bridged the divide between sectarian violence and spiritual action. This new book by Heathcote Williams not only contains that life but reflects its achievements in the shine of Thin Man Press' ninety beautifully packaged pages.

The hands and hearts of both Williams and Khan have been joined in this book, along with all of those who accompanied and continued the struggle against ignorance and oppression. The wound, if not healed, now shines through.

To you then, as the potential readers of this seminal examination of a life's dedication and to its author, Heathcote Williams I offer a final Pashtun phrase, as quoted in the text:

Stre Mashe:

(Trans) May you never grow tired.

29/4/15

PROPOSAL FOR A TELEVISION SERIES ABOUT CHRISTOPER 'KIT' MARLOWE
by Heathcote Williams

The Pitch:

Who was Christopher 'Kit' Marlowe? "Marlowe comes closest to knowing Lucifer. Marlowe is God, and only God can make a Lucifer, and he's the one I can live for and with."

(Letter to Allen Ginsberg from Gregory Corso).

Marlowe was a force of nature; the leading writer of his day, state enlisted spy, atheist and proselytising homosexual, and probably the inspiration and teacher of William Shakespeare.

Dead at 29, Kit was an impassioned, volatile, brash genius. He virtually invented a vital, seminal new drama which held up a mirror to the hypocrisies and cruelty of Elizabethan society, and not only examined the forces that eventually formed the theatre we know today, but also the kind of society we have constructed for ourselves. He was the first to give theatre a voice, a voice the public applauded and other playwrights recognized. He was dangerous and revolutionary, and clearly had to be put down.

Henry VIII had killed over 70,000 of his own people. The Tudors were vicious, blood-thirsty Empire builders. Elizabeth I was Henry's daughter. Thirty people a week were executed during her reign, and the Queen herself is recorded as having taken a morbid interest in various 'new' inventions for torture instigated by her spymaster, Walsingham and torturer in Chief, Richard Topcliffe.

The very first plays to challenge the prevailing culture were written by Marlowe, described by the Victorian poet Swinburne as Shakespeare's John the Baptist.

Marlowe was instinctively transgressive, but it was his membership in Sir Walter Raleigh's School of Night (also known as the School of Atheists), alongside such notables as the discoverer of Jupiter's moons and that helped forge the threat he posed to the Elizabethan mindset.

His surveillance was undertaken for obvious reasons: he fiercely castigated England's war economy and the theocracy which sought to justify it. He favoured science instead of superstition; he was anarchic rather than deferential; he risked both life and liberty to satirize the tyranny of corruption which he saw as dominant; he tore into Catholics and Puritans alike and defied the hierarchical and monarchical superstitions of the day.

Shakespeare would make free use of what Ben Jonson called 'Marlowe's mighty line' and Marlowe's invention became Shakespeare's most invaluable template, the DNA of a newly accessible dramatic verse.

Hazlitt on Marlowe: "There is a lust of power in his writings, a hunger and thirst for unrighteousness, a glow of the imagination, unhallowed by anything but its own energies."

KILLING KIT would be the first series to place Christopher Marlowe at the core of Elizabethan England and to have an openly gay figure as that protagonist. Adapted from his visceral play of the same name the projected series, Heathcote Williams examines the various suspects believed to be responsible for Marlowe's eventual murder, alongside evocations of his greatest theatrical successes. Marlowe's connection to the high and low ends of Elizabethan culture are exposed, forging a series as dramatically engaging as it is educational. Written with a vital and poetically charged language it lifts historical drama out of the period ghetto and places it firmly within the realms of contemporary relevance.

Divided into six parts each episode details a different element of Marlowe's career, from Poet, Playwright, Spy, Revolutionary, Fugitive and Martyr. The murder mystery elements popular in today's Television drama are transposed to the Elizabethan age and the hypocrisy and duplicitous venality and corruption of that time are writ large. This is not Elizabethan as we have come to expect it, but probably nearer the truth. The story is not about the assumption of Kings and Queens, but rather the perversion of political power incidentally laying waste to the innovations of art. It also puts Shakespeare and his achievements in a quite different light.

So, why Marlowe? He threatened the entire system. He was anti-war, scathing of religion, a voracious homosexual and practitioner of the unmentionable sin of sodomy of which, as William Empson said, "despite the punishment of death Marlowe believed that it was the only proper thing to do."

A Poet and Streetfighter, Marlowe was also the herald of a more modern and scientific age and of the kind of society that celebrates freedom of thought.

A series whose protagonist's very existence calls into question the basic tenets of the society in which he lives, is as fresh and revolutionary today as it was in Elizabethan England. The parallels with today are easy to see and will have tremendous resonance with today's audience.

Prepared by Heathcote Williams, Tony Palmer and David Erdos 24/3/16

Photo by David Erdos

David Erdos is an actor, writer, director, teacher, artist and filmmaker, and has worked closely with Heathcote Williams, Alan Moore, Snoo Wilson, Ian Sinclair, and a vast array of counter-cultural figures. He is the literary editor of *Mu* magazine and the forthcoming *The Return to Reason* series for Bitesize Books, and a regular contributor to *IT: International Times, The Magazine of Resistance*. Previous books include *The Scar on the Cloud, Oil on Silver* and, with photographer Max Reeves, *Byzantium*.

Printed in Great Britain
by Amazon

44433273R10051